Table of Contents

Useful Telephone Numbers

FOR INFORMATION ON DIPLOMATIC AND CONSULAR PERSONNEL AND PERSONNEL OF INTERNATIONAL ORGANIZATIONS OTHER THAN THE UNITED NATIONS

DURING BUSINESS HOURS (8 A.M. – 5 P.M. EST)

Current status of U.S. Department of State driver licenses, diplomatic license plates, registrations, or other diplomatic motor vehicle information:	(202) 895-3521 Fax: (202) 895-3646
For reporting traffic incidents or accidents, issuance of citations, etc., involving foreign missions personnel:	(202) 895-3521
Send all citations and/or reports to:	Fax: (202) 895-3646
To verify immunity status:	(202) 647-1985 or (202) 647-1727

PLEASE SEND COPIES OF CRIMINAL INCIDENT REPORTS AND CITATIONS TO:

The Office of the Chief of Protocol	Fax: (202) 647-1198
Diplomatic Security Service Protective Liaison Division	Fax: (202) 895-3613

AFTER BUSINESS HOURS

After business hours, all inquiries should be made to the U.S. Department of State Diplomatic Security Command Center (operates 24-hours daily):	(571) 345-3146 or toll free 1-866-217-2089

TO VERIFY THE IMMUNITY STATUS OF UNITED NATIONS PERSONNEL

DURING BUSINESS HOURS (8 A.M. – 5 P.M. EST)

Diplomatic agents and family members, UN Mission staff and family members, and UN Secretariat employees	(212) 415-4168 or (212) 415-4407 or (212) 415-4131
U.S. Department of State license tags, registration, or other motor vehicle information:	(646) 282-2825 or (646) 282-2812

AFTER BUSINESS HOURS

Information is available from the Communications Section of the U.S. Mission to the United Nations (USUN - operates 24-hours daily)	(212) 415-4444

U.S. DEPARTMENT OF STATE • BUREAU OF DIPLOMATIC SECURITY • OFFICE OF FOREIGN MISSIONS

Preface

INTERNATIONAL LAW, TO WHICH THE UNITED STATES is firmly committed, requires that law enforcement authorities of the United States extend certain privileges and immunities to members of foreign diplomatic missions and consular posts. Most of these privileges and immunities are not absolute, and law enforcement officers retain their fundamental responsibility to protect and police the orderly conduct of persons in the United States. This booklet provides a guide to the categories of foreign mission personnel and the privileges and immunities to which each is entitled. It explains how to identify (and verify the identity of) such persons and furnishes guidance to assist law enforcement officers in the handling of incidents involving foreign diplomatic and consular personnel.

I
Introduction

WHAT IS DIPLOMATIC IMMUNITY? Diplomatic immunity is a principle of international law by which certain foreign government officials are not subject to the jurisdiction of local courts and other authorities for both their official and, to a large extent, their personal activities.

The principle of diplomatic immunity is one of the oldest elements of foreign relations. Ancient Greek and Roman governments, for example, accorded special status to envoys, and the basic concept has evolved and endured until the present. As a matter of international law, diplomatic immunity was primarily based on custom and international practice until quite recently. In the period since World War II, a number of international conventions (most noteworthy, the Vienna Convention on Diplomatic Relations and the Vienna Convention on Consular Relations) have been concluded. These conventions have formalized the customary rules and made their application more uniform.

Notwithstanding the antiquity of the concept of diplomatic immunity, its purpose is often misunderstood by the citizens of this and other countries. Occasional abuses of diplomatic immunity, which are brought to public attention, have also served to prejudice public attitudes toward this practice. Dealing with the concept of immunity poses particular problems for law enforcement officers who, by virtue of their oath and training, are unaccustomed to granting special privileges or concessions to individuals who break the law. On the other hand, police officers who understand the importance of diplomatic immunity may be inclined to be overly generous in its application if they do not have a full understanding of its parameters. It is the purpose of this booklet to familiarize police officers with the general rules of diplomatic and consular immunity and to provide them with specific guidance regarding the handling of difficult situations.

The term diplomatic immunity is popularly, and erroneously, understood to refer to special protections afforded all employees of foreign governments who are present in the United States as official representatives of their home governments. Law enforcement officials, however, must have a more sophisticated understanding of the concept. There are over 100,000 representatives of foreign governments, including dependents, in the United States. Many of these persons may be entitled to some degree of immunity under international law. Some of these persons are members of diplomatic missions, others are assigned to consular posts, and still others are employees of international organizations or members of national missions to such international organizations. For each of these categories of persons, particular rules apply and, even within these categories, different levels of immunity may be accorded to different classes of persons. Most of these persons are assigned to Washington, D.C., and New York City, but large numbers are assigned in other major cities around the country. Moreover, nearly all of these persons are free to travel around the country either on official business or for pleasure.

II
Legal and Practical Basis of Immunity

THE SPECIAL PRIVILEGES AND IMMUNITIES accorded foreign diplomatic and consular representatives assigned to the United States reflect rules developed among the nations of the world regarding the manner in which civilized international relations must be conducted. The underlying concept is that foreign representatives can carry out their duties effectively only if they are accorded a certain degree of insulation from the application of standard law enforcement practices of the host country. The United States benefits greatly from the concept as it protects US. diplomats assigned to countries with judicial systems far different than our own.

The various categories of immunity are explained below (and a table is provided to summarize elements of paramount concern to law enforcement officials (on Page 27)), but all have a common legal foundation. While customary international law continues to refine the concepts of diplomatic and consular immunity, the basic rules are currently embodied in international treaties. These treaties have been formally adopted by the United States and are, therefore, pursuant to the US. Constitution, "the supreme law of the land." The U.S. Government is legally bound to ensure that such privileges and immunities are respected by its states and municipalities.

US. law regarding diplomatic immunity has its roots in England. In 1708 the British Parliament formally recognized diplomatic immunity and banned the arrest of foreign envoys. In 1790 the United States passed similar legislation which provided absolute immunity for diplomats, their families and servants, as well as for lower ranking diplomatic mission personnel. This 1790 law remained in force until 1978, when the present Diplomatic Relations Act (22 U.S.C. 254) was enacted to replace it.

The principal purpose of the 1978 Act was to bring U.S. law into line with the 1961 Vienna Convention on Diplomatic Relations (which entered into force for the United States in 1972). The 1978 Act imposed a more precise regime and reduced the degree of immunity enjoyed by many persons at diplomatic missions.

On a practical level, failure of the authorities of the United States to respect fully the immunities of foreign diplomatic and consular personnel may complicate diplomatic relations between the United States and the other country concerned. It may also lead to harsher treatment of U.S. personnel abroad, since the principle of reciprocity has, from the most ancient times, been integral to diplomatic and consular relations.

It should be emphasized that even at its highest level, diplomatic immunity does not exempt diplomatic officers from the obligation of conforming with national and local laws and regulations. Diplomatic immunity is not intended to serve as a license for persons to flout the law and purposely avoid liability for their actions. The purpose of these privileges and immunities is not to benefit individuals but to ensure the efficient and effective performance of their official missions on behalf of their governments. This is a crucial point for law enforcement officers to understand in their dealings with foreign diplomatic and consular personnel. While police officers are obliged, under international customary and treaty law, to recognize the immunity of the envoy, they must not ignore or condone the commission of crimes. As is explained in greater detail below, adherence to police procedures in such cases is often essential in order for the United States to formulate appropriate measures through diplomatic channels to deal with such offenders.

III

Categories of Persons Entitled to Privileges and Immunities

MEMBERS OF DIPLOMATIC MISSIONS

Diplomatic missions are traditionally the principal communication link between the country that sends them and the host country. Accordingly, the staffs of diplomatic missions (embassies) are afforded the highest level of privileges and immunities in the host country in order that they may effectively perform their important duties. Under modem international law (reflected in the Vienna Convention on Diplomatic Relations), however, there are different categories of persons within each diplomatic mission, some of whom enjoy greater immunities than others.

The categories of diplomatic mission personnel are defined primarily with reference to the functions performed.[1] Diplomatic agent is the term for ambassadors and the other diplomatic officers who generally have the function of dealing directly with host country officials. This category enjoys the highest degree of immunity. The next category is "members of the administrative and technical staff" of the mission, which includes those persons who support the activities of diplomatic agents. This category includes secretaries, certain clerical personnel, office managers, and certain professional security personnel. Members of the administrative and technical staff enjoy privileges and immunities which in some respects are less than diplomatic agents. Finally, there are the "members of the service staff" of the diplomatic mission who perform tasks such as driving, cleaning, and/or grounds maintenance. These persons are afforded significantly less in the way of privileges and immunities. The privileges and immunities of each of these groups is explained in more detail below, and a table is provided to summarize the privileges and immunities of greatest interest to law enforcement personnel.[2] Also provided is an explanation of important exceptions to the general rules. (A discussion of tax and customs duty exemptions and other privileges not of immediate concern to law enforcement and judicial authorities is not included in this booklet.)

Diplomatic Agents. Diplomatic agents enjoy the highest degree of privileges and immunities. They enjoy complete personal inviolability, which means that they may not be handcuffed (except in extraordinary circumstances), arrested, or detained; and neither their property (including vehicles) nor residences may be entered or searched. Diplomatic agents also enjoy complete immunity from the criminal jurisdiction of the host country's courts and thus cannot be prosecuted no matter how serious the offense unless their immunity is waived by the sending state (see discussion below). While it is not ordinarily of concern to police authorities, they also have immunity from civil suit except in four very limited circumstances: (a) in connection with real property transactions not conducted on behalf of the mission; (b) in connection with any role they may play as executor for or heir to an estate being distributed in the host country; (c) in connection with the performance of professional or commercial activities outside the scope of their official duties; or (d) in respect of counterclaims on the same subject matter when they have been the initiating party in a suit. Finally, they enjoy complete immunity from the obligation to provide evidence as witnesses and cannot be required to testify even, for example, if they have been the victim of a crime.

Family members forming part of the household of diplomatic agents enjoy precisely the same privileges and immunities as do the sponsoring diplomatic agents.[3]

Members of Administrative and Technical Staff. Members of the administrative and technical staff of a diplomatic mission perform tasks critical to the inner workings of the embassy. Accordingly, they enjoy privileges and immunities identical to those of diplomatic agents in respect of personal inviolability, immunity from criminal jurisdiction, and immunity from the obligation to provide evidence as witnesses. Their immunity from civil jurisdiction, however, is quite different. Members of the administrative and technical staff enjoy immunity from civil jurisdiction only in connection with the performance of their official duties. This is commonly known as official acts or functional immunity and is explained in more detail in the section below addressing consular privileges and immunities.

Like those of diplomatic agents, the recognized family members of administrative and technical staff enjoy the same privileges and immunities from the host country's criminal jurisdiction as their sponsors. Since these family members have no official duties to perform, they enjoy no immunity from civil jurisdiction.

Members of Service Staff. Members of the service staff of diplomatic missions perform less critical support tasks for the missions and are accorded much less in the way of privileges and immunities than are those in the other categories. Service staff members have official acts immunity only (see further explanation below) and they enjoy no personal inviolability, no inviolability of property, and no immunity from the obligation to provide evidence as witnesses. The families of service staff members enjoy no privileges or immunities.

Nationals or Permanent Residents of the United States. The general rules set forth above assume that the staff members of the diplomatic mission are nationals of the sending country or some third country. The United States, as a matter of policy, does not normally accept as diplomatic agents its own nationals, legal permanent residents of the United States, or others who are "permanently resident in" the United States.[4] The family members of diplomatic agents enjoy no privileges or immunities if they are nationals of the United States. Members of the administrative and technical staff (including their families) and members of the service staff enjoy no privileges and immunities if they are U.S. nationals, legal permanent residents, or foreign nationals "permanently resident in" the United States.

Police officers should not have to deal with this distinction since the U.S. Department of State issues identification cards (see further discussion below) with the nationality principle in mind. However, it is important for law enforcement officials to understand these principles generally, because they could confront a situation wherein a U.S. citizen spouse of a foreign national diplomatic agent (who lacks the correct identity documents) attempts to establish his or her immunity solely on the basis of proving a relationship with the diplomatic agent.

Special Bilateral Agreements. There are some countries with which the United States has concluded bilateral agreements which grant to all members of the staff of their respective embassies (provided that they are nationals of the sending country) the privileges and immunities to which only diplomatic agents are normally entitled. Identification cards will reflect this status but police officers should be aware of this distinction because they may have to confront situations where a chauffeur or mechanic from the embassy of one of these countries asserts a right to full diplomatic privileges and immunities.

Temporary Duty. Persons sent to the United States on short-term official duty with diplomatic missions ordinarily do not enjoy any privileges and immunities (law enforcement authorities should nonetheless always seek prompt verification from the U.S. Department of State in particular cases involving such individuals).

Waiver. Always keep in mind that privileges and immunities are extended from one country to another in order to permit their respective representatives to perform their duties effectively; in a sense, it may be said the sending countries "own" these privileges and immunities. Therefore, while the individual enjoying such immunities may not waive them, the sending states can, and do. Police authorities should never address the alleged commission of a crime by a person enjoying full criminal immunity with the belief that there is no possibility that a prosecution could result.

The U.S. Department of State requests waivers of immunity in every case where the prosecutor advises that, but for the immunity, charges would be pursued. In serious cases, if a waiver is refused, the offender will be expelled from the United States and the U.S. Department of State will request that a warrant be issued and appropriate entries to the National Crime Information Center (NCIC) database be made by the responsible jurisdiction. The seeking of waiver of immunity is handled entirely via diplomatic channels, but effective and informed police work becomes the basis of the prosecutor's decision and the foundation for the U.S. Department of State's waiver requests and any subsequent prosecutions or expulsions.

MEMBERS OF CONSULAR POSTS
(NORMAL AND SPECIAL BILATERAL)

Consular personnel perform a variety of functions of principal interest to their respective sending countries (e.g., issuance of travel documents, attending to the difficulties of their own nationals who are in the host country, and generally promoting the commerce of the sending country). Countries have long recognized the importance of consular functions to their overall relations, but consular personnel generally do not have the principal role of providing communication between the two countries — that function is performed by diplomatic agents at embassies in capitals. The 1963 Vienna Convention on Consular Relations grants a very limited level of privileges and immunities to consular personnel assigned to consulates that are located outside capitals.

There is a common misunderstanding that consular personnel have diplomatic status and are entitled to diplomatic immunity.

Consular Officers. Consular officers are those members of consular posts who are recognized by both the sending and the host country as fully authorized to perform the broad array of formal consular functions. They have only official acts or functional immunity in respect of both criminal and civil matters and their personal inviolability is quite limited. Consular officers may be arrested or detained pending trial only if the offense is a felony and that the arrest is made pursuant to a decision by a competent judicial authority (e.g., a warrant issued by an appropriate court).[5] They can be prosecuted for misdemeanors, but remain at liberty pending trial or other disposition of charges. Property of consular officers is not inviolable. Consular officers are not obliged to provide evidence as witnesses in connection with matters involving their official duties, to produce official documents, or to provide expert witness testimony on the laws of the sending country. Absent a bilateral agreement, the family members of consular officers enjoy no personal inviolability and no jurisdictional immunity of any kind.

As indicated, official acts immunity pertains in numerous different circumstances. No law enforcement officer, State Department officer, diplomatic mission, or consulate is authorized to determine whether a given set of circumstances constitutes an official act. This is an issue which may only be resolved by the court with subject matter jurisdiction over the alleged crime. Thus, a person enjoying official acts immunity from criminal jurisdiction may be charged with a crime and may, in this connection, always be required to appear in court (in person or through counsel). At this point, however, such person may assert as an affirmative defense that the actions complained of arose in connection with the performance of official acts. If, upon examination of the circumstances complained of, the court agrees, then the court is without jurisdiction to proceed and the case must be dismissed. Law enforcement officers are requested to contact the Department of State before arresting a consular officer, or, if not possible, immediately after arrest.

Consular officers who are full-time practitioners of consular functions are referred to as "career" consular officers. These officers are normally nationals of the sending country who are sent to the United States to perform these functions for a specific period and then are transferred to a further assignment. Career consular officers are prohibited by international law from engaging in professional or commercial activities outside the scope of their official consular functions.

Consular Employees. Consular employees perform the administrative and technical support services for the consular post. They have no personal inviolability, only official acts immunity, and enjoy immunity from the obligation to provide evidence as witnesses only in respect of official acts. Their family members enjoy no personal inviolability or jurisdictional immunities of any kind.

Consular Service Staff. Consular service staff do not enjoy personal inviolability or jurisdictional immunity of any kind, but they do have immunity from the obligation to provide evidence as witnesses in respect of official acts. Their family members enjoy no personal inviolability or jurisdictional immunity of any kind.

Nationals or Permanent Residents of the United States. Consular employees and consular service staff who are U.S. nationals, legal permanent residents, or who are permanently resident in the United States enjoy no personal inviolability or jurisdictional immunity in the United States. (See endnote 4)

Honorary Consuls. Honorary consuls are American citizens or permanent resident aliens who perform consular services on a part-time basis. Honorary consuls, unlike career consuls, are permitted to carry on another business. These persons have "official acts" immunity only and immunity from the obligation to provide evidence as witnesses only in respect of official acts. They do not enjoy personal inviolability and may be arrested pending trial if circumstances should otherwise warrant. Family members enjoy no immunity or personal inviolability.

Honorary consuls are issued official identification cards by the Department of State.

Special Bilateral Agreements. In some cases, a country and the United States have concluded a bilateral consular agreement that grants to members of the staff of their consulates (provided they are not U.S. nationals, legal permanent residents, or permanently resident in the United States) privileges and immunities approximating those afforded diplomatic agents. Law enforcement officers should be aware that these arrangements are not uniform and the State Department identification cards issued to these persons reflect the appropriate level of immunity.

Temporary Duty. Persons sent to the United States on short-term official duty with diplomatic missions ordinarily do not enjoy any privileges and immunities (law enforcement authorities should nonetheless always seek prompt verification from the U.S. Department of State in particular cases involving such individuals).

Waiver. As is the case with members of the staffs of diplomatic missions, the sending country may always waive the privileges or immunities of members of its consular posts. This is less likely to be an issue for consular personnel, however, since their immunities are so limited.

INTERNATIONAL ORGANIZATION PERSONNEL AND NATIONAL MISSIONS TO SUCH ORGANIZATIONS

International organizations, such as the United Nations, are relatively modern entities. The privileges and immunities of the personnel of such organizations and the personnel of national missions to such organizations have a different basis than that of diplomatic and consular representatives. In the case of international organizations, the nations concerned have agreed that the important purposes of such organizations may be accomplished only if a certain measure of privileges and immunities are afforded to their participants. The nations concerned have concluded treaties embodying such grants of privileges and immunities. Some, including the United States, enacted domestic legislation granting specific privileges and immunities to certain categories of persons not covered by the treaties. In determining the degree of inviolability or immunity, law enforcement officers will be guided primarily by the identity documents that have been issued to such persons. The following, however, provides a general overview of the distribution of privileges and immunities in connection with international organizations.

Personnel of International Organizations. International organizations that have headquarters or other offices in the United States are staffed with administrative and executive employees, as necessary, to carry out their functions. The vast majority of these employees enjoy only official acts immunity as provided for in U.S. domestic legislation (the International Organizations Immunities Act, 22 U.S.C. 2881) and no personal inviolability. In certain cases, however, the most senior executives of such organizations have been accorded privileges and immunities equal to those afforded diplomatic agents. This is the case for the Secretary General of the United Nations and for all Assistant Secretaries-General of the United Nations, Principal Resident Representatives of the International Monetary Fund and the World Bank, as well as some senior officials of the Organization of American States secretariat.

Personnel of National Missions to International Organizations. The United Nations and the Organization of American States are headquartered in the United States, and most of their member States maintain permanent missions to the headquarters in the United States. The permanent representatives staffing these missions are accredited to the international organization concerned (not to the United States), but their privileges and immunities are nonetheless often defined by reference to the status of diplomatic personnel who are accredited to the United States.

As is the case with diplomatic missions, the assignment of privileges and immunities is differentiated generally on the basis of the functions performed. The most senior representatives in these missions to international organizations have privileges and immunities equivalent to those afforded diplomatic agents. The remainder of the staffs of these missions have only official acts immunity pursuant to the International Organizations Immunities Act and no personal inviolability.

Short-term official visitors from other States to the United Nations or to international conferences convened by the United Nations may enjoy full diplomatic immunity equivalent to that afforded diplomatic agents. Owing to the temporary nature of their visit, such officials will normally not have the usual official identity documents recognizable in the United States. Law enforcement officials (particularly in New York) should be sensitive to the existence of this situation and always coordinate with the U.S. authorities indicated in the list of Useful Phone Numbers if confronted with an apparent offender appearing to fall into this category.

[1] The definition of these categories is general since the category into which specific individuals fall may differ depending on reciprocal practices with the countries concerned. Law enforcement personnel, however, do not need to worry about these distinctions in operational situations. Their responsibility is to assure that the appropriate degree of immunity is afforded once the person concerned has been precisely identified.

[2] The private servants of diplomatic personnel enjoy no jurisdictional immunity or inviolability in the United States.

[3] The United States defines members of the household to include: spouses, children until the age of 21 (until the age of 23 if they are full-time students at an institution of higher learning), and such other persons expressly agreed to by the U.S. Department of State in extraordinary circumstances.

[4] A member of a mission, other than a diplomatic agent, "permanently resident in" the United States for purposes of Article 38(2) of the VCDR and Article 71(2) of the VCCR enjoys no privileges and immunities pursuant to the Vienna Conventions.

[5] Police officers should note this distinction carefully. In connection with other categories discussed in this booklet, either a person is absolutely protected from arrest or, alternatively, he or she has no immunity from arrest whatsoever. In the case of career consular officers, such arrest may be carried out only if the police officer is operating under the authority of a warrant or similar judicial authorization. Note, however, the discussion below of the public safety prerogatives of police authorities.

IV

Identification of Persons Entitled
to Privileges and Immunities in the United States

IT IS CRITICAL FOR A LAW ENFORCEMENT OFFICER to identify quickly and accurately the status of any person asserting immunity. Numerous documents are associated with foreign diplomats; only one provides an accurate indication of the status of the holder. This section endeavors to explain the array of documents and clarify for police officers which one may be relied upon.

IDENTIFICATION CARDS ISSUED BY THE U.S. DEPARTMENT OF STATE

The only authoritative identity document is the identity card issued by the U.S. Department of State's Office of Protocol, or by the U.S. Mission to the United Nations in the case of persons accredited to the United Nations. There are three types of identification cards (see sample cards beginning on page 23): Diplomatic (blue border for diplomats), Official (green border for embassy employees), and Consular (red border for consular personnel). The identification cards are 3⁷⁄₁₆" x 2³⁄₁₆" and contain a photograph of the bearer. The bearer's name, title, mission, city and state, date of birth, identification number, expiration date, and a U.S. Department of State seal appear on the front of the card. A brief statement of the bearer's criminal immunity is printed on the reverse side. Space is provided for the bearer's signature. While this form of identification is generally to be relied upon, law enforcement authorities are nonetheless urged to immediately seek verification as indicated below in connection with any serious incident or in any case where they have reason to doubt the validity of the card. Police officers should be alert to the fact that newly arrived members of diplomatic and consular staffs may not yet have these official identity documents and should contact the U.S. Department of State's Office of Protocol for verification if confronted with such situations.

FOREIGN DIPLOMATIC PASSPORTS
AND U.S. "DIPLOMATIC" VISAS: NOT CONCLUSIVE

Foreign diplomatic passports containing U.S. "A" or "G" visas are issued to a broad range of persons, including those who are not accredited to the United States or to international organizations and who therefore enjoy no privileges and immunities in the United States.[6] This situation is often not fully understood, even by the bearers of such documents, so police officers must be alert to good faith, but erroneous, assertions of immunity by those not entitled to it.

The possession of these documents is an indication that the bearer might be entitled to privileges and immunities in the United States. As mentioned above, temporary duty visitors to the United Nations might have only such documents and might nonetheless be entitled to immunity in the United States. A similar situation could arise in connection with the foreign officer who has just joined a diplomatic mission or consular post and has not yet received the appropriate U.S. identity documents. In cases of doubt, police officers should always coordinate with U.S. authorities on the list of Useful Phone Numbers.

TAX EXEMPTION CARDS: NOT CONCLUSIVE

Under international law, many members of diplomatic missions and consular posts and certain people associated with international organizations would normally be entitled to exemption from sales taxation in the United States. However, significant numbers of these individuals do not enjoy this privilege owing to considerations based on reciprocity. The U.S. Department of State issues tax exemption cards to all those entitled to such exemptions, but tax cards do not give a definitive indication of the degree of immunity of the bearer. (See sample tax exemption cards on page 25.) Accordingly, tax exemption cards should not be relied upon for immunity purposes and should be considered only as an indication that the bearer may enjoy some degree of immunity.

AUTOMOBILE REGISTRATION, LICENSE PLATES, AND DRIVER LICENSES: NOT CONCLUSIVE

The U.S. Department of State, through its Office of Foreign Missions' Diplomatic Motor Vehicle Office, has jurisdiction over the registration of vehicles, the issuance of distinctive license plates for those vehicles, and the issuance of operator permits for individuals who enjoy privileges and immunities in the United States. (See sample Non-Driver ID and Driver License cards on page 26.) As is the case with tax exemption cards, these federal registration documents and driver licenses do not definitively reflect the degree of privileges and immunities of the bearer. They should be relied upon only as an indication that the bearer may enjoy some degree of immunity. Vehicle license plates issued by the U.S. Department of State must be understood properly by law enforcement authorities in order to avoid confusion. The plates are coded to reflect the degree of immunity which the registered owner of the vehicle enjoys:

- Plates with a "**D**" prefix or suffix are issued to diplomatic missions and those members who hold diplomatic rank.

- Plates with a "**C**" prefix are issued to consular missions and career consular officers.

- Plates with a "**S**" prefix are issued to the administrative and technical staff at diplomatic missions and consular employees at consular missions.

- Plates with an "**A**" prefix or suffix are issued to official vehicles of the Secretariats of the United Nations and the Organization of American States and the personally owned vehicles of those staff members who have diplomatic status.

The U.S. Department of State's distinctive license plates are designed to assist officers in identifying vehicles that belong to foreign missions and those mission members who may enjoy some degree of immunity. However, those plates alone should not be considered verification of the status of the vehicle's operator. For example, police officers should bear in mind that a diplomatic agent who is visiting a consulate may be driving a car with "C" plates. Or a U.S. citizen who is the spouse of a diplomat may be driving a car with "D" plates even though he or she does not have immunity. (Conversely, a diplomatic agent or consular officer may be driving a rented or borrowed car that does not have any type of U.S. Department of State license plate.) These examples serve to emphasize that, whatever kind of license plate is on a vehicle, police officers need to verify with the Department of State's Office of Protocol a driver's claim of diplomatic or consular status.

A vehicle registration card is issued at the time of initial registration and registration renewal. It contains the following information: name and address of the registered owner, license plate number, vehicle identification number, vehicle make, vehicle model, vehicle color, date of initial registration, and expiration date of the current registration. Decals with the month and year reflecting the expiration date of the current registration period are issued with the card and must be displayed on the vehicle's rear license plate.

The U.S. Department of State's vehicle registration and driver license status records are available to law enforcement agencies through the National Law Enforcement Telecommunications System (NLETS). Agencies may access these records using the standard NLETS registration and driver query formats. NLETS has assigned state code (destination ORI) "US" to this data base. If an agency requires additional motor vehicle information, it can be obtained telephonically (see list of Useful Phone Numbers, page v) or by sending an administrative message to "DCDOS015V."

TELEPHONIC INFORMATION/VERIFICATION

In all cases, including those in which the individual provides a U.S. Department of State-issued identification card, the law enforcement officer should verify the immunity status with the U.S. Department of State.

Department of State representatives are available 24-hours daily to assist in emergency situations and when immediate confirmation of a person's status is required. The telephone numbers provided on page v are for use in such instances.

[6.] All foreign personnel assigned to official duty at bilateral diplomatic or consular missions in the United States would have A-category visas. G-category visas are issued to foreigners assigned to duty at an international organization in the United States or at a foreign country's mission to such organization.

V
Terms and Procedures

CORRECT UNDERSTANDING OF IMMUNITY

Frequently (and erroneously), immunity is understood to mean pardon, total exoneration, or total release from the responsibility to comply with the law. In actuality, immunity is simply a legal barrier which precludes U.S. courts from exercising jurisdiction over cases against persons who enjoy it and in no way releases such persons from the duty, embodied in international law, to respect the laws and regulations of the United States. Even those who properly understand the concept of immunity sometimes erroneously believe that it is senseless to waste valuable police time in the investigation and paperwork essential to building a legal case on the assumption that there is no possibility that a conviction will result. However, there are diplomatic remedies available to deal with such persons even when immunity bars prosecution and conviction. As explained below, there are a number of important reasons for police authorities to give careful attention to the documentation of incidents involving persons enjoying privileges and immunities. Such incidents should always be promptly reported to the U.S. Department of State.

PERSONAL INVIOLABILITY VS. PUBLIC SAFETY

Personal inviolability is enjoyed to some degree by a majority of foreign diplomatic and consular personnel. This inviolability generally precludes handcuffing, arrest, or detention in any form and forbids U.S. authorities from entering the residences, automobiles, or other property of protected persons. Personal inviolability is, however, qualified by the understanding, well established in international practice, that the host country does not give up its right to protect the safety and welfare of its populace and retains the right, in extraordinary circumstances, to prevent the commission of a crime.

Thus, in circumstances where public safety is in imminent danger or it is apparent that a grave crime may otherwise be committed, police authorities may intervene to the extent necessary to halt such activity. This naturally includes the power of the police to defend themselves from personal harm.

WAIVER OF IMMUNITY

Diplomatic and consular immunity are not intended to benefit the individual; they are intended to benefit the mission of the foreign government or international organization. Thus an individual does not "own" his or her immunity and it may be waived, in whole or in part, by the mission member's government. The U.S. Department of State will request a waiver of immunity in every case in which the prosecutor advises that he or she would prosecute but for immunity. The U.S. Department of State's ability to secure such waiver may depend to a large degree on the strength (and documentation) of the case at issue. Similarly, it is of little avail for the U.S. Department of State to secure a waiver of immunity in a particular case, if the case has not been developed with sufficient care and completeness to permit a successful subsequent prosecution. Proper documentation and reporting by law enforcement authorities plays a critical role in both of these respects.

EXPULSION PROCEDURE

The criminal immunity that foreign diplomatic and some consular personnel enjoy protects them from the normal jurisdiction of the courts with respect to alleged criminal activity. However, in those instances in which a person with immunity is believed to have committed a serious offense (any felony or crime of violence) and the sending country has not acceded to the U.S. Department of State's request for a waiver of immunity, it is the Department's policy to require the departure of that individual from the United States. Requiring the departure of a person who enjoys immunity is an extreme diplomatic tool, and it is used only after the most careful consideration to ensure that the United States is not perceived as having acted in an arbitrary, capricious, or prejudiced manner. A high standard of police investigation, records, and reporting in diplomatic incident cases is therefore essential to permit the Department to make the appropriate decision.

OFFICIAL ACTS IMMUNITY

As explained in Section III, official acts immunity is not a prima facie bar to the exercise of jurisdiction by U.S. courts. Rather, it is an affirmative defense to be raised before the U.S. court with subject matter jurisdiction over the alleged crime. Only such court, in the full light of all the relevant facts, determines whether the action complained of was an official act. Should the court determine that official acts immunity applies in a certain case, international law precludes the further exercise of jurisdiction by the United States. Judicial determination in a case of this type is very much dependent on the facts surrounding the incident; therefore, a full and complete police report may be critical in permitting the court to make a just decision.

TERMINATION OF IMMUNITY

Criminal immunity precludes the exercise of jurisdiction by the courts over an individual whether the incident occurred prior to or during the period in which such immunity exists. This jurisdictional bar is, however, not a perpetual benefit. With the exception of immunity for official acts (which exists indefinitely), criminal immunity expires upon the termination of the diplomatic or consular tour of the individual enjoying immunity. Therefore, obtaining an indictment, information, or arrest warrant could lay the basis for a prosecution at a later date, e.g., if the diplomat returns to the United States at a later date in a private capacity. Moreover, the existence of an outstanding arrest warrant may be entered into the records of the National Crime Information Center (NCIC) and thus serve to bar the subsequent issuance of a U.S. visa permitting such person to enter the United States.

ARCHIVES

The archives and official documents of a diplomatic or consular post are inviolable at all times and wherever they may be. The consular archives and documents of a consular post headed by an honorary consular officer are inviolable provided they are kept separate from other papers and documents of a private or commercial nature relating to other activities of an honorary consular officer or persons working with that consular officer.

VI
Handling Incidents

U.S. DEPARTMENT OF STATE POLICY

It is the policy of the US. Department of State with respect to alleged criminal violations by persons with immunity from criminal jurisdiction to encourage law enforcement authorities to pursue investigations vigorously, to prepare cases carefully and completely, and to document properly each incident so that charges may be pursued as far as possible in the US. judicial system.

The U.S. Department of State will, in all incidents involving persons with immunity from criminal jurisdiction, request a waiver of that immunity from the sending country if the prosecutor advises that but for such immunity he or she would prosecute or otherwise pursue the criminal charge. If the charge is a felony or any crime of violence, and the sending country does not waive immunity, the U.S. Department of State will require that person to depart the United States and not return unless he or she does so to submit to the jurisdiction of the court with subject matter jurisdiction over the offense. Upon departure, the Department will request that law enforcement issue a warrant for the person's arrest so that the name will be entered in NCIC.

GENERAL PROCEDURES

The vast majority of persons entitled to privileges and immunities in the United States are judicious in their actions and keenly aware of the significance attached to their actions as representatives of their sending country. On occasion, however, one of them may become involved in criminal misconduct. The more common violations are traffic (illegal parking, speeding, reckless driving, and DWI), shoplifting, and assault.

Whatever the offense or circumstances of contact, law enforcement officers should keep in mind that such persons are official representatives of foreign governments who are to be accorded the maximum degree of respect possible under the circumstances. It is not an exaggeration to say that police handling of incidents in this country may have a direct effect on the treatment of US. diplomatic or consular personnel abroad.

When a law enforcement officer is called to the scene of a criminal incident involving a person who claims diplomatic or consular immunity, the first step should be to verify the status of the suspect. Should the person be unable to produce satisfactory identification and the situation be one that would normally warrant arrest or detention, the officer should inform the individual that he or she will be detained until his or her identity can be confirmed. In all cases, including those in which the suspect provides a U.S. Department of State-issued identification card, the law enforcement officer should verify the status with the U.S. Department of State or, in the case of the UN community, with the U.S. Mission to the United Nations. Once the status is verified, the officer should prepare his or her report, fully describing the details and circumstances of the incident in accordance with normal police procedures. If the suspect enjoys personal inviolability, he or she may not be handcuffed, except when that individual poses an immediate threat to safety, and may not be arrested or detained. Once all pertinent information is obtained, that person must be released. A copy of the incident report should be faxed or mailed as soon as possible to the U.S. Department of State in Washington, D.C., or to the U.S. Mission to the UN in New York in cases involving the UN community. Detailed documentation of incidents is essential to enable the U.S. Department of State to carry out its policies.

TRAFFIC ENFORCEMENT

Stopping a mission member or dependent and issuing a traffic citation for a moving violation does not constitute arrest or detention and is permitted. However, the subject may not be compelled to sign the citation. In all cases, officers should follow their departmental guidelines and document the facts of the case fully. A copy of the citation and any other documentation regarding the incident should be forwarded to the U.S. Department of State as soon as possible. For "must appear" offenses, the Department uses the citation and any report as the basis for requesting an "express waiver of immunity." Individuals cited for pre-payable offenses are given the option of paying the fine or obtaining a waiver in order to contest the charge.

In serious cases, e.g., DWI, DUI, personal injury, and accidents, telephonic notification to the U.S. Department of State is urged. The officer should follow his or her department's guidelines with respect to the conduct of a field sobriety investigation. If appropriate, standardized field sobriety testing should be offered and the results fully documented. The taking of these tests may not be compelled. If the officer judges the individual too impaired to drive safely, the officer should not permit the individual to continue to drive (even in the case of diplomatic agents). Depending on the circumstances, there are several options. The officer may, with the individual's permission, take the individual to the police station or other location where he or she may recover sufficiently to drive. The officer may summon, or allow the individual to summon, a friend or relative to drive; or the police officer may call a taxi for the individual. If appropriate, the police may choose to provide the individual with transportation.

The U.S. Department of State's Diplomatic Motor Vehicle Office maintains driver histories on all its licensees and assesses points for moving violations. Drivers who demonstrate a pattern of bad driving habits or who commit an egregious offense such as DWI are subject to having their licenses suspended or revoked as appropriate. This policy can be enforced effectively only if all driving infractions (DWI, DUI, reckless driving, etc.) are reported promptly to the U.S. Department of State. It is U.S. Department of State policy to assign "points" for driving infractions and to suspend the operator license of foreign mission personnel who abuse the privilege of driving in the United States by repeatedly committing traffic violations and demonstrating unsafe driving practices.

The property of a person enjoying full criminal immunity, including his or her vehicle, may not be searched or seized. Such vehicles may not be impounded or "booted" but may be towed the distance necessary to remove them from obstructing traffic or endangering public safety. If a vehicle that is owned by a diplomat is suspected of being stolen or used in the commission of a crime, occupants of the vehicle may be required to present vehicle documentation to permit police verification of the vehicle's status through standard access to NLETS (use access code US). Should the vehicle prove to have been stolen or to have been used by unauthorized persons in the commission of a crime, the inviolability to which the vehicle would normally be entitled must be considered temporarily suspended, and normal search of the vehicle and, if appropriate, its detention, are permissible.

Vehicles registered to consular officials, including those with full criminal immunity, and consulates are not inviolable and may be towed, impounded, or booted in accordance with local procedures. The U.S. Department of State should be notified if a consular vehicle has been detained or impounded so that its Office of Foreign Missions can follow up with the proper consular official or mission.

Federal license plates issued by the U.S. Department of State are not the property of the diplomat or of a diplomatic mission and remain the property of the Department at all times. As such, they must be surrendered to the U.S. Department of State when recalled. Similarly, these license plates may not be transferred from the vehicle to which they were assigned by the U.S. Department of State without the authorization of its Office of Foreign Missions.

In cases where the officer at the scene has determined that the vehicle is being operated without insurance and/or has verified with the U.S. Department of State that the vehicle bearing U.S. Department of State license plates is not the vehicle for which those plates were intended, the Department may request that the local law enforcement agency impound the plates and return them to the Department. Such impoundment should only be upon the request of the U.S. Department of State. Subsequent detention of the vehicle must conform to the guidelines above.

VII
Conclusion

IT IS IMPORTANT THAT LAW ENFORCEMENT and judicial authorities of the United States always treat foreign diplomatic and consular personnel with respect and with due regard for the privileges and immunities to which they are entitled under international law. Any failure to do so has the potential of casting doubt on the commitment of the United States to carry out its international obligations or of negatively influencing larger foreign policy interests. As stated above, however, appropriate caution should not become a total "hands off" attitude in connection with criminal law enforcement actions involving diplomats.

Foreign diplomats who violate traffic laws should be cited. Allegations of serious crimes should be fully investigated, promptly reported to the U.S. Department of State, and procedurally developed to the maximum permissible extent. Local law enforcement authorities should never be inhibited in their efforts to protect the public welfare in extreme situations. The U.S. Department of State should be advised promptly of any serious difficulties arising in connection with diplomatic or consular personnel. Law enforcement and judicial authorities should feel free to contact the U.S. Department of State for general advice on any matter concerning diplomatic or consular personnel.

VIII
Examples: Identifying Documents

U.S. DEPARTMENT OF STATE IDENTIFICATION CARDS

The United States Department of State's Office of the Chief of Protocol, issues identification documents to foreign government personnel who are entitled to immunity. Samples of the identification cards are provided here. Because there are different degrees of immunity, law enforcement officers should read carefully identification cards presented to them. During business hours (8 a.m. – 5 p.m. EST) questions regarding an individual's status or immunity should be referred to the Office of Protocol at (202) 647-1985. After business hours, please contact the Diplomatic Security Command Center at (571) 345-3146 or toll-free at 1-866-217-2089.

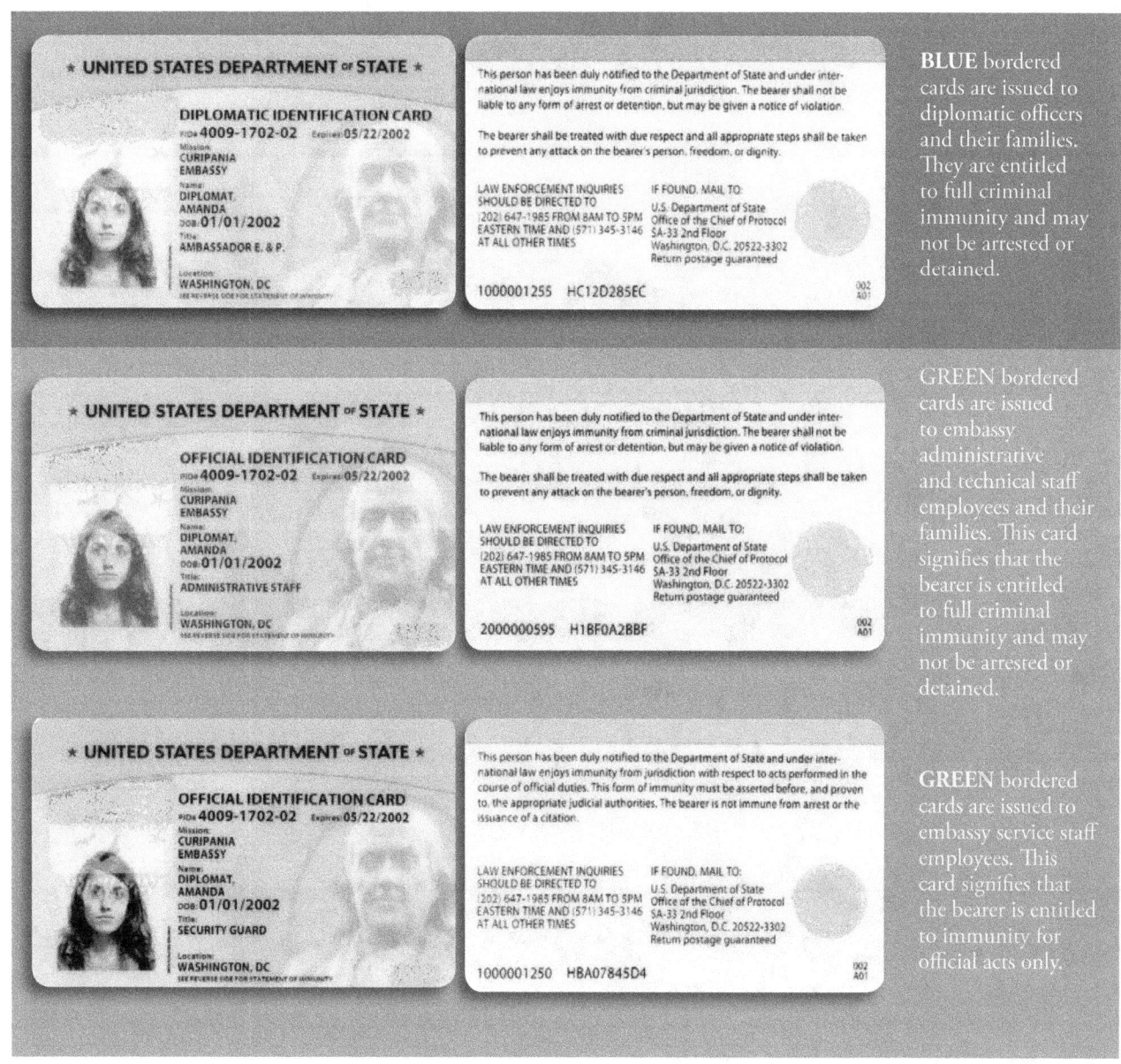

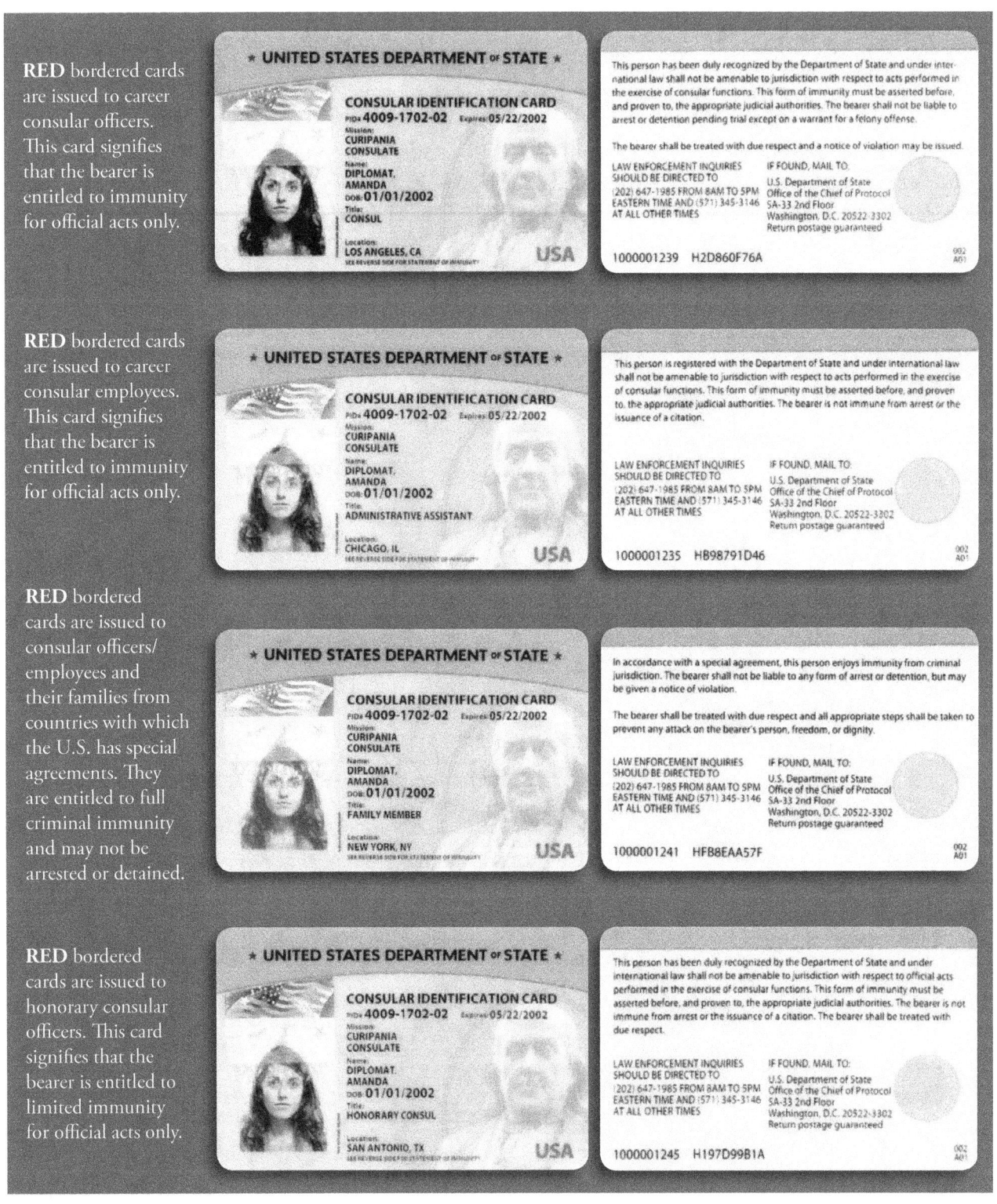

RED bordered cards are issued to career consular officers. This card signifies that the bearer is entitled to immunity for official acts only.

RED bordered cards are issued to career consular employees. This card signifies that the bearer is entitled to immunity for official acts only.

RED bordered cards are issued to consular officers/ employees and their families from countries with which the U.S. has special agreements. They are entitled to full criminal immunity and may not be arrested or detained.

RED bordered cards are issued to honorary consular officers. This card signifies that the bearer is entitled to limited immunity for official acts only.

U.S. DEPARTMENT OF STATE TAX EXEMPTION CARD

Diplomatic Tax Exemption Cards are designed with state of the art security features that are intended to defeat any attempts to manufacture counterfeit versions of these cards. These features include, but are not limited to, the use of laser-engraved personalization of data, the inclusion of an optically variable device or Kinegram, and tactile micro-text (small raised text).

U.S. DEPARTMENT OF STATE DRIVER LICENSE AND NON-DRIVER ID

Description: Background colors on the front are powder blue fading to pink image of Lincoln Memorial interior; lettering is black, with gold OFM logo in bottom right corner. U.S. Department of State driver licenses are designed with state of the art security features that are intended to defeat any attempts to manufacture counterfeit versions of these cards. These features include, but are not limited to, the use of laser-engraved personlization of data, the inclusion of an optically variable device or Kinegram, and tactile micro-text (small raised text).

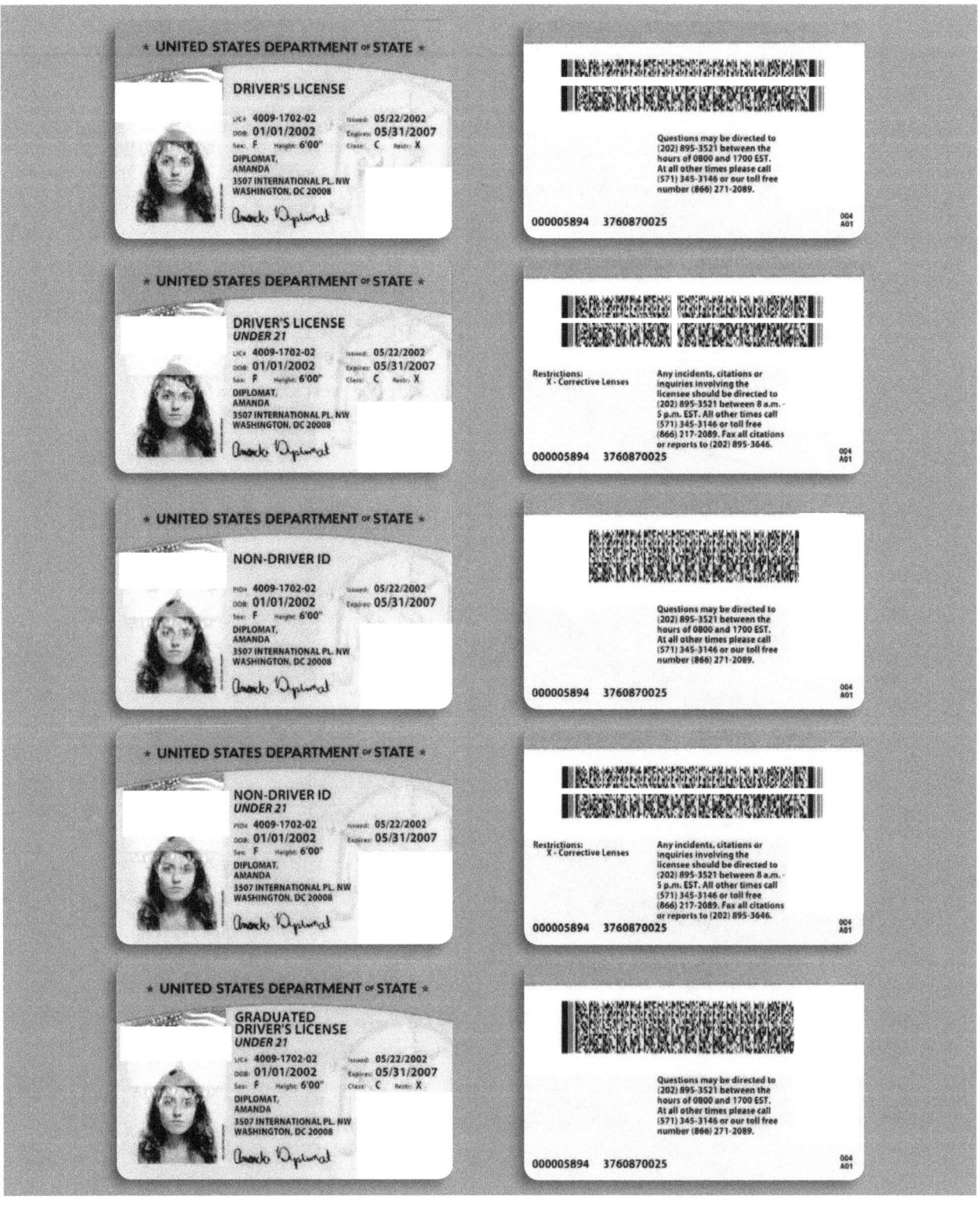

SAMPLES OF U.S. DEPARTMENT OF STATE-ISSUED DIPLOMATIC AND UNITED NATIONS MISSIONS LICENSE PLATES

DIPLOMATIC MISSIONS

UNITED NATIONS

DIPLOMATIC AND CONSULAR PRIVILEGES & IMMUNITIES FROM CRIMINAL JURISDICTION
LAW ENFORCEMENT ASPECTS SUMMARY

	Category	Arrested or Detained?	Enter Residence Subject to Ordinary Procedures?	Issued Traffic Citation?	Subpoenaed as Witness?	Prosecuted?	Recognized Family Member?
International Organizations	International Organization Staff[3]	Yes	Yes	Yes	No—for official acts. Yes, in all other cases.	Official acts immunity. Consult Dept. of State.	No immunity or inviolability.
	Diplomatic-Level Staff of Missions to International Organizations	No[1]	No	Yes	No	No	Same as sponsor (full immunity and inviolability).
	Support Staff of Missions to International Organizations	Yes	Yes	Yes	No—for official acts. Yes, in all other cases.	Official acts immunity. Consult Dept. of State.	No immunity or inviolability.
Diplomatic	Diplomatic Agent	No[1]	No	Yes	No	No	Same as sponsor (full immunity and inviolability).
	Member of Administrative and Technical Staff	No[1]	No	Yes	No	No	Same as sponsor (full immunity and inviolability).
	Service Staff[2]	Yes	Yes	Yes	Yes	Official acts immunity. Consult Dept. of State.	No immunity or inviolability.
Consular	Career Consular Officers[2]	No, except in the case of a felony and pursuant to a warrant.	Yes[4]	Yes	No—for official acts. Testimony may not be compelled in any case.	Official acts immunity. Consult Dept. of State.	No immunity or inviolability.
	Honorary Consular Officers	Yes	Yes	Yes	No—for official acts. Yes, in all other cases.	Official acts immunity. Consult Dept. of State.	No immunity or inviolability.
	Consular Employees[2]	Yes	Yes	Yes	No—for official acts. Yes, in all other cases.	Official acts immunity. Consult Dept. of State.	No immunity or inviolability.

[1] Reasonable constraints, however, may be applied in emergency circumstances involving self-defense, public safety, or the prevention of serious criminal acts.

[2] This table presents general rules. The employees of certain foreign countries may enjoy **higher** levels of privileges and immunities on the basis of special bilateral agreements.

[3] A small number of senior officers are entitled to be treated identically to "diplomatic agents."

[4] Note that consular residences are sometimes located within the official consular premises. In such cases, **only** the official office space is protected from police entry.

Direct questions or inquiries to the Diplomatic Security Command Center.

Call **571-345-3146** or Toll free to **1-866-217-2089**

Available 24 hours daily

CONSULAR NOTIFICATION

Assistance with consular notification procedures following the arrest or detention of a foreign national.

Business hours: 202-647-4415

After-hours: 202-647-1512

Fax Number: 202-647-7559

IMMUNITY ISSUES

Contact the Office of Protocol: Diplomatic Affairs

202-647-1727

www.ingramcontent.com/pod-product-compliance
Lightning Source LLC
Chambersburg PA
CBHW081249170526
45165CB00009B/3251